# "You're Standing On My Foot"

## by Howard Paris

**Warner Press**
**Anderson, Indiana**

PRINTED IN THE UNITED STATES OF AMERICA

I HOPE I DON'T HAVE THAT MUCH TROUBLE GETTING INTO HEAVEN

I BELIEVE IN TRAINING FOR WITNESSING

I TAKE EVERY EVANGELISM STUDY COURSE I CAN GET

IN FACT, I'VE BEEN STUDYING FOR YEARS

ONE OF THESE DAYS I'LL HAVE TO PUT SOME OF IT INTO PRACTICE